SHATTERPROOF:

The Art of Perseverance

Dr. Kendrick Carroll, DBA

For information or speaking engagements please email info@drkcarroll.com.

ISBN-13: 978-0-578-64671-8

This book is dedicated to my wife, son, brother, and sister, whom I love so dearly. Thank you for all of your support during my endeavors. It is my hope and wishes that my efforts encourage each of you to continue to strive for your goals.

To my beautiful mother, I know you are resting well in heaven. I love you and hope I have and will continue to make you proud.

To my dear brothers of our great fraternity, Omega Psi Phi, thank you for helping me see the real value in my perseverance.

CONTENTS

PREFACE

   "ShatterProof – The Art of Perseverance" is a combination of inspirational stories based on my life journey thus far. I was exposed to significant amounts of domestic violence while living in poverty with my mother and siblings. At the age of 11, I lost my mother at the hands of her husband, who later killed himself. This traumatic event brought about significant changes in my life at a very early age. In the years after losing my mother, I became a victim of child abuse, immersed in gang activity, and acquired the stigma of being the poor, ignorant motherless black boy. Despite what others thought of me, I knew I was destined for something greater. The stigma placed on me by others was my past. I was determined to ensure it was not my future.

   I am writing this book to encourage all of my readers to persevere through any obstacles they are facing. I am sure others have faced situations similar to the ones I am going to share with you. The fear of judgment has silenced so many, including me. What I have learned over the years is that you cannot fix what you do not know. I am sharing my story and efforts to overcome the challenges I've experienced in life in hopes of sparking a change in every reader of this book.

This book will take you on my journey from when I was a menace to the point; I made a definitive decision to make a change. Throughout this journey, you will experience some of the pain I have endured. You will see the tears I cried. You will experience my trauma, and you will be privy to the circumstances that shaped my character. I hope that my story inspires you to persevere.

CHAPTER 1

INTRODUCTION

S tarting as a youngster, I found my first challenge in life. I was different, with no real explanation as to why. I would look around at other individuals in hopes of finding any common traits. As I looked around with curiosity, I realized I lacked a majority of all the commonalities of others from my appearance and hobbies to my desires and aspirations. Not just with friends or associates, but even in my relationship with family members. Somehow, someway my outlets and inlets were structured differently from those around me. The majority of my immediate influencers were smokers, alcoholic drinkers, and individuals with entirely different hobbies from mine. At times I felt as if I was in a world alone.

There were very few people to talk to for general purpose and almost no one to talk about my thoughts and feelings. So, over some time, I acquired a stoic mindset. I learned to suppress my thoughts and feelings to channel them in a different direction when I was alone. It was a robust approach, and people may even wonder why. For me, I had already experienced massive trauma in life, and those who I expected to support me were non-existent. So, for me, I did not have the time nor interest to worry and convince individuals of my needs, I had responsibilities. My two other siblings needed me, and I refused to let either of them down. So, I focused on a different goal. But before I get too deep into my responsibilities, let me lay a portion of my family foundation for you.

My mother was murdered when I was 11 years old by her husband on Memorial Day, 1998. Before the death of my mother, my dad was around on the 1st and 3rd weekends. He had a new family in Warner Robins, Georgia, that seem to prevent him from visiting or spending time with us on any additional days. However, after the tragic event that occurred on Memorial Day, my brother and I was forced to go live with him and his new family.

We will talk more about that situation in more detail in a later chapter; let's say he was there but not there for me at the same time (Daddy versus Father…there is a difference). As for siblings, there were three of us. My older brother and baby sister. My older brother and I have the same parents; my baby sister, on the other hand, had a different dad. However, we do not see a difference; we are blood brothers and sisters, period.

Growing up, my brother and I were extremely close. We joke about it often, but it was freakishly close when we look back over time. We spent almost every minute of the day around each other. Our first day apart was not until he entered the Armed Forces.

We, as kids, shared the same friends, and the funny part about it is, we still do. However, I found my brother's passions to be total opposites of mine. He enjoyed fishing and computers while I was loving sports and trying to figure out life. His relationship with our dad was strong, while mine, well, it was non-existent. The way things happened differently with my dad, I sincerely questioned whether or not he was my father. It was like there was going to be this big secret that comes out later in life that I was adopted or birthed out of infidelity. You will understand more about the abnormality of our relationship in a later chapter.

As for my sister, she was indeed a life changer for me. She is truly the reason I gained a profound level of respect for accountability and responsibility at an early age. My brother and I made a vow to our mother. When our sister was born, to take care of and protect her at all cost. Never did we know or imagine that we would have to elevate that level of protection and to care so soon.

It was strange, to say the least, growing up in my life. Things always felt unfair or intentionally uneven. I was born with nowadays would be called a congenital disability. I was born with 12 fingers and a heart defect. Accompanying those different traits was more teasing and taunting from others. I'm talking about things that people would be laughing hysterically over, but hurt me to my core. To add insult to injury, when people found out that I was from a broken home with my mother; the tormenting became overwhelming. It was at this stage in my life where I was introduced to the true meaning of poverty.

We lacked the natural things in life, for instance, hot water and consistent heat. I used the term comfortable because we've learned that you can still survive in this life without them. It's not recommended, but you get the point. The lack of heat created one of my greatest memories with my mother. I remember it was a cold morning; my mother had to turn on the radiator heater in the house, and for us to feel the warmth, we had to stand directly in front of it. Well, she and I were booty bumping trying to move the other person from in front of the heater; that was a pretty cool memory for me.

As an adult, I realized that these were actions she took not to make memories with me, but to also, keep my mind off of us lacking certain things that others had. There were numerous times where we did not have hot water in our home, so my mother would run a half tub of cold water, while she boiled a pot of hot water on the stove. Once all was completed, she would mix it all to give us a chance to bathe in warm water.

My brother and I would have to share the same water to keep from having to take a cold bath. Sounds strange to some and familiar to others; but hey, what can I say, that was our life. It taught us the values in small things in efforts for us to appreciate all things.

Lacking financial resources forced us to live on the most dangerous street in Macon, GA, Fort Hill. Fort Hill was notorious for massive drug trafficking and murder. Imagine hearing gunshots daily or walking outside of either door of your home to find drugs being sold or cooked (made). That's was my life. This environment introduced me to gang life at an early age. At nine years old, I experienced my first gang fight and my first drive-by shooting: good ole Davis Homes, our projects.

Due to domestic violence, my living conditions were consistently unstable. Whether it was physical or verbal abuse, there was always some form of disruption occurring. My mother's husband was still at the center of it. He would get drunk and jump on her as if she was some animal on the street.

I remember seeing and hearing the brutal beatings and me trying to defend my mom. Imagine a small skinny kid trying to fight a grown drunk man; it was insane. Then, after all of the shenanigans were over, she would leave and take us to our grandmother's house, but over time, we would always end up back in the hell hole of life. It was like our lives were hand-carved by the devil. He was determined to take us through pure chaotic hell.

If it was not domestic violence, it was the teasing I received as a result of being less fortunate or being perceived as ignorant due to my lack of institutional knowledge. As an adult, I now understand the reason for my lack of education.

How in the heck can a person learn in these types of environments?

My illiteracy prevented me from understanding what was happening in my life and the course I was on. I was confined to a world consumed with fearless emotions and violence. It was my lack of knowledge and comprehension that prohibited me from knowing how to pronounce or even spell my first name until the 6th grade. I was so consumed with my environment that I failed all of elementary school, 1st – 5th grade. I was expelled in fourth grade for excessive fighting and weapons.

As I think about the struggles, I realized that I was a kid torn by violence. The only avenue I knew to express myself was violence, so when all else failed, that is where I turned to for an escape. There was no peace at home. I was forced to live in survival and protection mode every day between those four walls. I was responsible for protecting my mother, brother, and my sister. I was a like a firecracker always lit, just waiting to explode.

Sometimes, it takes losing something near and dear to you to save your life. For some strange reason, that is what the murder of my mom did for me. It did not happen overnight. As you continue to read, you will see I had several more ups and downs over the years. After losing my mother, we were forced to stay with my father. His life to us was completely different.

I mean for us seeing him and his new family, it was like they had it all, especially to kids who struggled with even taking a hot bath or having consistent heat in the home. Soon enough, I realized that the grass was not greener on the other side. My brother and I were looked at as the poor motherless boys. Hell, we were already written off before we even started. Fortunately for my brother, people were more supportive and believed he had a stronger probability of doing something with his life. Me, on the other hand, well, you will see as we dive deeper into my story. Everyone had written me off to prison or dead by the age of 20. Very optimistic, I know!

People who have met me at the age of 18 or older, mostly imagine me as a different type of person who is always optimistic. Many times, we judge a book by its current cover, but that is because we were not privy to the cover before the upgrade. I hope the cover of this book depicts a clear picture of what you will see on the inside, pain, struggle, determination, inspiration, and perseverance.

By no means is this book designed to predict your future or tell you how to live your life. What it is intended for is to share a story of a person doomed to failure but found success on a difficult journey. It is my hope and prayer that through my words, a deposit is made into your life to encourage and inspire you to push through whatever adversity you might be facing. I hope to encourage all of you to take your deposit from me and place it into the lives of our youth. Your deposit can be what changes the next little me. I hope something or many things from my story connect with you very well. Happy reading!

CHAPTER 2

SHARD

So, who am I? Well, that's a loaded question. For most, I'm probably known as a serial entrepreneur, instructor, drill sergeant, Que, or just an energetic individual hungry for success. All of which is true, but these images were probably formed from a previous encounter with my current self, whether in person, on TV, radio, or over social media. However, others who've only known my past would argue differently.

Dr. Kendrick Ra'Shard Carroll is my full name, but for those who knew me as a troubled youth, remember me as Shard. The boy who cared nothing about consequences and was fearless when it came to authority. I know you are probably wondering how is this quick snippet relevant here, well, let me get straight to the point.

From as early as I can remember, the only name I knew of was Ra'Shard. Every document I signed or saw with my information listed Ra'Shard as my first name. Because of this, I could not spell or even reference my first name, Kendrick, until 6th grade. During this time, I was, let's say, a unique individual. No one, inside nor outside my family, could view, speak, or even imagine a positive outcome on my life. I was a real-life problem child. Some would even venture to say, a parent's worst nightmare. How come you asked? Well, let me explain.

By the age of 8, I had developed an uncontrollable temper. From the hectic living conditions at home to the project lifestyle, it seemed impossible to balance proper behavior. I was introduced to the gang life while living in the projects of Davis Homes in Macon, Georgia. By the time I entered 3rd grade, I had experienced my first gang fight. It was during this same year and time that I experienced my first drive-by shooting, all within the same environment. Let me paint a quick picture for you.

It was just a typical day in the projects when an old grey chevy caprice went speeding up the Maynard Street, and shots begin to ring out. I just stood there watching until my mom immediately pushed me into the apartments for protection. At that time, I finally realized, my fears were not like others. The fear of me losing my life was non-existent. Living in the projects and under certain conditions, you were forced to acquire a level of confidence, courage, and tenacity that no one could take from you. I guess that was a positive outcome from having that lifestyle. I was so far at the bottom that there was nothing to look down to, so I had to walk with my head high because, in my eyes, everything was already above me.

My temper was out of control. I was young, wild, dangerous, and lacked any emotional connection to anything other than the protection of my family. I was the youngest out of my brother and I. We were extremely close to my female cousins who also grew up with us. Our cousins were like our sisters. Neither hell nor high water could keep me from protecting them. I used to fight always during school hours after school hours, all in efforts to protect them, and they would do the same for us.

Being raised in the type of environment, we came from, this is the type of mindset I figured I needed for my family and me to survive. All we knew was a struggle. We went from struggling while living with my grandmother to, struggling while living in the worst part of Macon, GA; Fort Hill. We lived in the middle of the trap house and gun violence headquarters of Macon. We did our best not to complain because my mother was doing the best, she could to provide for us despite our living conditions and low income.

My mother worked as a home health nurse. She would travel to patient homes to treat their medical needs. As I think about it, that was a pretty unique job to have, especially after seeing some of the conditions of some of her patients. You want to talk about perseverance; those individuals were real Soldiers. We will go deeper into her career field in later chapters of the book.

Back to the topic at hand, Shard. It was a challenge growing up without real guidance and direction. The daily turmoil of gang life, poverty, and domestic violence was sure to lead me down a dead-end road. At an early age, I acquired a terrible habit. Some would call it sticky fingers, but let's keep it simple and straight to the point, I was stealing. The teasing from other kids on how less fortunate we were got the best of me. I was so sick of being the poor kids. I began to acquire things that did not belong to me. It started with a cupcake from my mom's purse (I know, it sounds fat, but hey!) All of the other kids at school would have an extra snack after lunch, but I could not afford one, so I took it. This incident led to many other instances. It went from snacks to money. It became a terrible habit that had to be stopped.

Once my mother found out about my extracurricular activities, it was on. She whipped my butt so bad, (whew) I never touched another thing that I could not afford. She took me to jail in Macon, where I had to spend one night in the cell. Remember when I told you all I was fearless, well that went out the window that night. I quickly realized that there was something in this world that I feared, jail. The experience is still blurry to me, but what I do remember is, my nerves were through the roof. Needless to say, the stealing immediately ceased, but the fighting, well that took more time.

After all of the chaotic events in the projects of Macon, we later moved out of the projects to a country town called Twiggs County. I went from watching drug deals and drive-by shootings to raising goats and rabbits. How does that work? Umm, I really do not know (lol). Subconsciously, I think there was an expectation that a better living would derive from this transition. However, the turn of events that occurred while in this country town was nowhere near better. During this time, my exposure to domestic violence increased. I was forced to watch a man brutally beat my mother day in and day out. As the domestic violence in the home worsened, so did my anger.

As I screamed and cried out for help, no one seemed to hear it or see it. All people could or wanted to see was my rage as it spilled over into my school life. It was as if my rage was louder than my screams. But in all actuality, my anger was fueled from the ignoring of my screams. Sometimes I wondered, did people not hear or see the pain I was enduring, or did they see it and chose to ignore it. Either way, I had to find a way to remain determined to defend my family.

My brother was older, but his temperament was mild. Me, on the other hand, I was always on fire, just ready to burst. My rage was so vicious that I ended up getting expelled from school in 4th grade, for excessive fighting and weapons. As I think about the times now, I was screaming for help but did not know how to ask for it properly. At home, I was fighting a grown man in efforts to get him off of my mom, and then I was going to school and fighting to defend my family from the cruel and harsh words of other students. Challenging is an understatement; this was pure hell. The final straw for me was an evening when things got out of control during the middle of the night. My mom's husband was just pounding away on her while we were sleeping.

The commotion awakened me, and that sent me over the edge. I started fighting this grown man as if I was an adult. I remember those words like it was yesterday; I said to him with the most conviction I could muster up, "It takes a boy to hit woman and man to walk away!" I was 11 years old when I stared down the barrel of a 9mm pistol held in his hand. He said to me, "little nigga, I'll kill you." My response, "well, I will die before I let you keep hitting my mom." My brother woke up in a panic as I stood beside the bed with a gun in my face. My mom stumbled in the room in an attempt to get in between her husband and me, that was the final straw for her. We finally moved away.

I know this sounds terrifying, and believe me, it was, but this is the reason I am writing this book. Others are experiencing very similar situations, and they are trying to find their way out of it. How do they overcome it, or do they give in to the environment? By no means do I have all of the answers or a blueprint for your life. What I do have are stories and testimonies of life experiences that have and are continuing to shape me into becoming a better person and man every day. My stories are not for glorification, but for encouragement for the readers to understand that life is made up of choices.

The question for any situation is not always about "what you did to get into this situation, but how do you overcome and get out of it?" Being Shard gave me plenty of reasons to give up and give into my environment. I chose, and I still intentionally select to keep fighting. Although I was unable to see what was beyond my current situation, somewhere deep inside of me, there was a fire that knew and convinced me that I was made for greater.

The one thing I knew for sure in my mind was, my life was in turmoil. The things I was experiencing were nowhere near better than those from people external to my family. So, I had nothing to lose, but everything to gain. I endured harassment as an impoverished youth and learned to accept my consequences at an early age while believing things would get better one day.

What is my point here? The life we are given or assigned may not be personally chosen by us, but it is designed exclusively for us. No one will ever be able to experience your life the way you have or will. So, when you think about your life compared to others, remember, you were made for this walk. Your strength has been evenly distributed to carry your life-load, just as others are strengthened for theirs. Stay encouraged and believe that there are greater things among you. Just keep persevering so that you can experience and enjoy the rewards from your struggle.

CHAPTER 3

I'M DIFFERENT

Being different in a contextual sense has gained a strong negative connotation over the years by judgmental individuals. This type of judgment has caused so many people to lose their strength and identity and has forced them to conform to the thoughts and views of others. I'm challenging the norm by saying it is perfectly ok to be different. We are all made equally. However, we are all different and unique in our way. I accept the fact that I am unique and different; because it has been the driving force for me to accomplish any goal that I set out to achieve.

We have all heard our parents or mentors tell us not to be followers but to be leaders; but our environments and fear of judgement negate those lessons before they are engraved in our psyche. As kids, we are encouraged to find a trade or something that we will want to do in life. Often times what we find has nothing to do with our passions because our parents have programmed us to believe that only specific roles can pay the bills.

How many times have you heard or seen a parent, or an adult stop a child from playing a video game to go and play outside? The majority of the reason is parents are afraid that the child will not be able to fit in with others or will lack the communication and social skills needed to function correctly. Well, playing video games can be more productive for the youth by unlocking talents and interests that can be later used in the Information Technology world. My point is, we have to learn to embrace our differences as well as the differences of others.

Due to my health condition as a youth, it limited my participation in organized sports activities. Despite my athletic abilities, the lack of confidence of others in my ability to overcome my medical condition crippled my chances of ever experiencing the joys of my life firsthand. I was born with a heart murmur, which caused many complications and obstacles for me. At an early age, I had two of my appendages removed. I was born with 12 fingers, and my mother was afraid of the ridicule I would have to undergo if I kept them, so she requested for my additional finger to be removed.

Unfortunately, the removal of my extra fingers did not stop the taunting from others. Somedays kids would say I had warts on my hands and on other days I had alien freak hands. (Pretty whack jokes, I know ☺). I was always the kid with the cooties; as we called it in the early 90's. Kids could be so mean at times. When others would have conversations about their sporting or family events, I would have to sit alone or create a story to fit in. The unfortunate part is, even with all of that lying, I still was never able to fit in. All of that hard work and fine-tuning to my lying abilities never paid off (☺).

Regardless of how I wanted to structure it or manipulate my mind, I was created differently. My purpose in this world was not the same as others. I was destined for something better. However, my environment would not allow me to see differently. Without the ability to see it, it was hard to recognize it, let alone accept it. Thus, the reason I gained a deeper understanding of the word "Faith,"; which you will understand in later chapters.

As unfortunate as it may seem, one of the greatest gifts that ever happen to me was my father ignoring my existence. At first, it was painful to cry for a person every day; until I finally got an opportunity with them and realized they never had an ounce of energy for me. I watched eagerly while my dad built a strong bond of love with his firstborn, hell he even put more effort into building a relationship with his stepdaughter.

It's crazy how it all unfolded. I mean, I watched them fish, drink, laugh, talk, and more while I sat alone trying to figure out who to turn to and which way to go.

It was as if what made me different made me unacceptable or unlovable to him. When it came down to activities or events, I could only participate in them if it involved something my brother or stepsister had previous engagement in. For some reason, my differences were damn near threatening to him.

The things I enjoyed doing, I had to do them alone. I was so lonely as a youth; I created imaginary friends while in high school to play basketball with me. (Pause) Do not judge me; we all have had those imaginary friends at some point in our lives; mine just stayed longer (laughing). I was not allowed to visit other people's homes who had kids my age. I was forbidden from having friends over, so I created people to spend time with me. As I reflect on this experience, it is very disturbing, but it's my journey.

I wanted to belong so badly I needed to feel like I fit in somewhere. Sometimes our desires to fit in drives us to make dumb decisions or to gain unwanted attention. For example, I used to think people who smoked looked cool. If there was one thing that I was sure of, it was that I wasn't cool, but I was about to be. I used to see people smoking all of the time and so did my dad, so I decided to tear up a brown paper bag and roll up pencil shavings and try to smoke it.

Yes, yes, yes, I know my impromptu "joint" was stupid and dangerous. I knew I wasn't going to be inhaling anything, I just wanted to look in the mirror to see how it felt to be "cool". Yea, I felt really dumb afterwards. Needless to say, it never happened again.

Why am I telling you this? Well, think about it. We are all faced with peer-pressure and other life situations that could drive an unintentional result. For years, we've been taught do not share what happens at home or in private. Well, I think that has become one of the most significant issues in America or at least within the African American culture. We've hidden so many life lessons from people that our openness has become critical. Often, by the time the person who needs the advice receives it, it is too late. So, I'm opening the doors to my life to share my experiences, mistakes, and growth opportunities for my readers to use for self-development or the development of others.

Another life-altering event for me was the gang life. Being initiated into a gang brought about a different reputation. Some may look at it as a terrible event, and probably you are right. For me, this was the only turn I was offered. Where does a young a kid find the support and strength to survive when even in your own home, it is dangerous? I turned to what I knew and leaned on it until I had enough power and desire to accept my differences. After a while, I found myself on a journey that I was not aware I was on.

The lesson for this story is, we all will face different circumstances in life that will sculpt our personality and character. We must learn to accept and embrace our differences and see them for what they indeed are, unique pieces of a puzzle to a beautiful masterpiece. Never be so quick to throw in the towel on yourself or someone else, just because things seem abnormal to you.

If the world was all made of the same structure, what would be the value? You see, things have to be different and changes have to take place in order to create the stories life has laid out for us. Life is all about the journey; if you are going through life just for the motions, I challenge you to start living.

The world is full of beautiful art, dare yourself to add your puzzle piece to the masterpiece of life. One final thing that I've learned, and I take with me every day is, it is those individuals who have not accepted being different that antagonizes others to satisfy their insecurity. But once you embrace your difference, it does not matter what the world thinks, because your vision will be different.

CHAPTER 4

BRENDA

or years I have yearned to hear her voice, to remember the sweet smell of her perfume or the gentle touch of her hand. The few memories of laughter we shared replay over and over in my mind as the years go by. The challenge with the life progression is, the memories become less and less detailed. I can see a face, but the image quality is low; it's like I'm looking at a pixelated image. I see pictures of her daily, but my memory of her is cloudy. I tend to speak about her less, because my memories of her are leaving as the details lessen.

I find myself crying at random times during the day because I'm not able to hear her voice. It's like an addict who needs a fix but there is nothing available. The only difference is, for an addict there are places where you can go to get help to overcome the illness; for me, there's no fix. When you are missing something that is such an intricate part of your life, and there is no substitution for it, it will tear away at you daily. Who is she you ask? Her name is Brenda Denise Mosely, the woman who gave me life, my forever queen, my mom!

Fortunately, she was an identical twin with my Aunt, who still carries the memories of her for me in her looks and some of her ways. To the best of my knowledge, my mom was a sweet and loving woman, who refused to take much from anyone. She was so sweet, but in the words of my grandmother, she was also feisty (lol).

It's funny as I write this book. I realized that a lot of my traits, especially my persistence and determination are qualities given to me through my mom. She worked multiple jobs to make ends meet for us. I recall in my shallow memory, her working at a local gas station called RaceTrac in Macon when I was a little boy. She would rent movies on a Friday evening for us all to watch over the weekend. It wasn't much, but when you come from nothing, all things count and have value. Boy Oh boy, those were some good times! Life without her has always been a challenge; however, I know being here on earth for her was not the best.

For years, I have always known that my mother was a victim of domestic violence. Hell, I was involved in several of those fights in an attempt to protect her. What I did not know until recently is, the domestic violence did not start with her most recent past husband, she was actually introduced to domestic violence by her first husband, my dad. When I first heard about this in 2019, it opened my eyes to a lot of things, but my dad being a woman beater, well, that was not surprising. His anger and temperament towards his wife and me always sparked questions in my mind. But in our culture, we have been taught to suppress and keep what happens in the house quiet. So, I have never had the courage to question things aloud.

It's amazing what you find out when someone gains the courage to talk. I've learned that if you take the time to study a person actions, you will uncover their true meanings, but be aware, you can also be influenced and confused by their words. At times I would daze off into space wondering and questioning, why was my mom unable to see the patterns. If she did see the patterns, what caused her to stay? I understand
love, but damn, the price we had to pay for love, I not sure if it was worth it, or was it?

Examining the tragedy of my mom opened doors that are hard to face, but I hope this encourages you to meet your challenges or fears head-on. On Memorial Day 1998, my mother was murdered by her husband in Twiggs County, GA. This tragedy taught me a valuable lesson that I believed shaped me into becoming the man that I am today.

So many times, I watched her be beaten bloody by her partner. From the fistfights between him and my mother, the brutal ass whippings he gave me for meticulous things or out of frustration, to the multiple kidnaps of my baby sister, there were lessons I gained from it all. When all of the beatings took place, she would convince us that she was going to leave, but the fear somehow held her back.

In life, we all face that same fear. Maybe it's not in the context of domestic violence but from some form of challenge in life. At this pivotal moment, you are giving a choice, whether you acknowledge it then or will in the future, the options are provided. You can either submit to the normality of the world or stand on your personal beliefs, morals, and values. It's not going to be easy but think about it…name one thing in this world that is easy to obtain, and through the ups and downs, it is worth holding. I can promise you there is nothing.

Everything that has value, you have to work for and earn. So, I encourage you to fight and push through. Do not allow the weight of the world or the opinions of others to keep you in something or somewhere that is not of value or in the best interest of you. You might not go for it all on the first time, but as long as you make progress each time, you are succeeding, and that's what matters. Personal growth is not measured in the eyes of others but in the eyes of the individual.

Take my mom's continuous progress as an example. Each time she was faced with an abusive situation, she gained a little more courage each go around. She went from saying, "I'm going to leave" to actually packing us up and moving out.

I'm not able to speak for her directly, but from my perspective, she was human and fell weak so many of times by going back. However, each time she went, she gained a little more strength. Finally, she built up enough strength and courage to leave for good. I was not in the room for the final conversation between her and her husband, but I want to believe that he asked her to come back. With the strength she'd gained from the previous incidents, she refused. This marked the words that sent him over the edge. Yes, it cost her the ultimate sacrifice, her life. Was it worth it? Well to her, I think it was. She provided peace on so many levels for her kids and herself.

What connection am I making? Well, sometimes you have to stand firm on what's right regardless of the price.

I'm not suggesting that you give up your life, but what I am suggesting is, help make a difference in the world by standing for what is right. Whether it's on your job, at home, or in a relationship, stand for what is right. If you get weak the first couple of times on your journey, it's ok, that means you are human ☺. Just pick yourself up and march forward stronger. You are not in a race with anyone else, only you.

As I wrote this chapter, I realized my mother deposited something in me that has fueled my journey and life purpose. She deposited in me unwavering faith, determination, and courage. With her deposits I've been able to persevere through various levels of adversity and challenges and that deposit continues to drive me forward on a daily basis. It's amazing what other people who are inspired by you can see. For instance, my brothers in the world's greatest fraternity, Omega Psi Phi, gave me the name ShatterProof. They were able to see a deposit in me that I was unable to see for myself. That's why it's said, nothing matters until you can see it and accept it for yourself.

I hope that my mom's deposit in me, and my story deposits something in you as you continue reading. I hope something that I've written inspires and motivates you to persevere and overcome any and every obstacle you desire. Remember, no matter how many times you fall, get back up. Do not worry about the dust you acquire; let it stay on; that's your masterpiece, titled perseverance.

CHAPTER 5

AVOID ONLY HE COULD FILL

Throughout earlier chapters, you've heard me touch on my relationship with my dad. I know your curiosity is brewing, so let's dive into it. Have you ever yearned for someone so bad, that you felt like you will give your all for them? Just for them to show you that you are not worth it to them. Well, that's kind of how things shaped out for me. I grew up in a broken home where communications between my parents were limited. I learned at a very early age how painful this could be. While living with my mom, I always had a strong desire to live with my dad. He was my rock, my security, my everything. To me, nothing else mattered as long as I could see him. Unfortunately, the feeling was never mutual. What do I mean? Well, let me explain.

It was at nine years old that I began to long for my dad. I was student at Jeffersonville Elementary School. I was selected for an award; I believe it was a for a field event, but it was something I tried very hard to achieve. When my teacher told me that I would be receiving an award, I was extremely excited because it was the only award I ever received as a youth. I remember coming home to my mom with so much excitement. I immediately asked her to allow me to call my dad. As I mentioned earlier, he was like everything to me. I called him with so much excitement in my voice and told him that I would be receiving an award and how bad I wanted to him to be there when I received it.

When I asked would he be there, he said yes, boy that made my day! The day finally came for the ceremony and I was so jazzed. I had butterflies flying all around in my stomach. My mom, brother, baby sister and cousin were all sitting in the audience; but for some reason I felt weird about everything. I didn't see my dad. I knew in my mind he would be there. I mean, every time my brother had an event, no matter how big or small it was, he was always there for him. I just knew when he said he would be there; he was a man of his word.

Time kept ticking away and I kept looking around trying to spot him, but I couldn't, and my excitement began to fade. Finally, it was time for me to walk up to receive my award and it hit me, he's not coming. I was stunned with disappointment. I've never won anything remotely close to an award, and the first time I did, I was left broken-hearted. When it was time to go up and accept the award, I stayed in my seat with a broken heart.

I couldn't understand it. He has never missed a single event for my older brother, why was he not there for me. It was at this moment I begin to wonder why me? I started to question things all around me. Why was my name different? Why was my older brother named after him and why did my name seemed to just have fallen out of the sky? He and my brother had a great relationship, but for some reason, he never really had a passion to build one with me. I wanted to be a daddy's boy so bad, but as I got older, I realized that just because you want something from someone else, doesn't mean they will want the same.

After being forced to go live with my dad after my mom was killed, my eyes were opened to a lot of things that my mother worked so hard to protect us from. When our mother was murdered, we grieved for months, but there was no one there to console us. My brother and I would hold each other while the tears ran down our faces as we questioned why us.

So many nights I wondered how am I in a house with the man that I've always wanted to be with, but he doesn't even notice that I'm hurting. With no hugs and no shoulder to cry on, we realized pain is pain, but it's hard to bear when you are hurting even more from being alone. I saw the connection between him and my brother get stronger and stronger over the years, but it was like hatred was forming for me. I started being punished for my differences early in life. I was whipped for every little thing I did or mistake I made.

What I did not understand and still do not entirely get is, how do consistently beat one child for something and never once spank the other one; no exaggeration, my brother has gone 30+ years without ever being punished by my dad. On the contrary, I've literally been brutally beaten by this man to the point I had to learn how to walk all over again.

At the age of 16, I was falsely accused of cursing at a student in JROTC. A program that I never wanted to be a part of, but I had to participate in it because my brother and my dad's stepdaughter was a part of it. The instructor called my dad and told him what I had been accused of doing. Immediately, I knew I was going to be in trouble. Never did I think it would end up the way it did. I came home from school and immediately went to the back yard where my father was to go ahead and address the issue that happened at school.

Before I could even say anything, the yelling and anger commenced. I express to him, I honestly did not say what I was accused of, but that did not go over well. At that moment I realized that I would rather stay any other place but there. I was tired of being cursed out, hit, degraded and belittled. I told him directly (not disrespectfully) that I wanted to stay with my grandmother.

Boy oh boy, that sent him way over the edge. By the time I was able to attempt to walk into the house, I was up in the air coming down on a concrete porch at the full force of an angry man. As I tried to get up, my stomach was met with several impacts from his boots. Into the grass I rolled. As I was attempting to gain my footing to stand, I realized my right leg not functioning. I immediately fell back to the ground with one final blow from him. I finally made my way to my feet with tears streaming down my face, screaming, don't kill me! I've never seen a person's eyes filled with so much anger as his eyes were that day, while he yelled at me at the top of his lungs. As I hopped into the house on my left leg, I immediately hit the floor after entering the door. I was in excruciating pain. My kneecap was on the right side of my leg, and my thigh and upper part of my lower leg were the same sizes.

For the first time in my life, I called 9-1-1 to report child abuse. When the cops arrived, I thought for sure they would help me; this was an open and shut case. You can clearly see what had happened. Well, the cop asked what happen, but the shocker in this situation was, they did not want to hear from me, they wanted his story. I will never forget his response, he told them, "I slipped and fell running into the house." Man, oh man, what kind of crap is this. That must have been one hell of fall! As soon as I said that was not true, the police told me to be quiet. He said, I look like the type that hangs with some other gang members, and if he did do this to me, I probably deserved it. My mind was blown! There was no way for me to win and get help here.

As my stepmother rushed me to the emergency room, I was met with my dad's mother, who continued where he left off and cursed me out. I swear, I can't make this stuff up. As the nurses were trying to get me out of the car and into a wheelchair, she was in my face, telling me I wasn't going to be shit, and I was going to hell for calling the police on my dad. Let's take a break and try to understand this because I still do not get it. How is that I'm getting beat and torn down, when I was lied on, brutally beaten, tried to do what was right, but I stilled end up in the wrong?

Well, news flash, sometimes life will take you on a journey that will seem like hell, all to give you the courage to persevere through life. The thing that was my greatest desire ended up being my greatest pain. However, despite the hardship I had to grow through. There was something in me that was greater and kept me pushing. I learned then to never depend on someone else to elevate you or protect you; you have to do it yourself.

If people do not want to be associated with you, cool, let them go. Why hold on to dead weight? I spent years of my adult age wasting time and running after significant accomplishments to make my dad recognize me, but nothing ever changed. What I realized during this time of chasing was never chase a person who is not willing to pursue you. You have a life and your life is just as important as anyone else's. When God created us all, he gave all of us unique characteristics. If someone does not see value in you, that's their lost not yours.

You walk on faith and determination in knowing you are more significant than any thought or opinion anyone else can formulate. Your life journey is yours, and you have come too far on this road to be trotted over or derailed by others' negativity. Encourage yourself, day-in, and day-out! Walk proudly with your head held high and chest out, knowing you are destined for greatness. Life does not have a one size shoe fit all model, so how can someone else walk in your shoes? If they can't walk in your shoes, there's absolutely no way for them to know your journey, so why listen to their negativity. Be you and be damn proud of being you!

CHAPTER 6

THE FIGHT

We are in a day and time where we can no longer hide the truth from our youth, and we have to find a way to teach them differently. Every day when I turn on the news, or I see a shared video on social media, I continuously see young kids fighting or even adults. If not fighting, then shooting or some form of an altercation. I would be a hypocrite if I were to tell everyone that I'm some perfect person or I was an absolute angel as a child, that would be a major lie.

What I am hoping for and the reason I'm putting these words on paper is to touch someone who will touch someone else to start changing how things are shaping up in our communities. When we see the word "Fight," it is usually accompanied by negative connotations. However, the truth is, fighting can represent negativity and positivity. It all depends on what, who, and why you are fighting. Let me explain.

After being introduced to domestic violence in the home, it was never really easy for me to express my feelings verbally. Each time I tried, it felt as if I was continuously misunderstood. I guess after so much violent trauma, you become numb to emotions and not being heard.

I remember times in my elementary school days, where I would ask a question to the teacher, and there would always be someone there to remind me of how dumb or poor I was. When my teacher did not make a statement or correct the situation, it often made me feel as if I was just as what kids called me. My grades began to decline significantly.

It was like I was trapped in a whirlwind tunnel. At home, things were chaotic, and when I came to school, things weren't any better. The distress and turmoil of a dysfunctional home don't just have an impact on the adults involved, but also it impacts the children that are exposed to it. It was at this point in my life where I started to find my comfort in the fighting.

I was guaranteed to get into at least one altercation weekly. I began bringing knives and metal nuts to school to wear on my knuckles to fight the older kids who would tease me, my brother, and cousins. I was in full rage mode. Fighting was my cry for help. I couldn't seem to find the words to express what I was going through. All I knew was, I wanted help, but I never understood how to ask for it. How does a person get up if all they know is down? I will tell you how I did it in the next chapter.

Fortunately, enough for me, I was never a disrespectful child. However, I was full of anger. I was a trauma filled balloon that would eventually pop. The unfortunate part for me and others was, my balloon was always full; so, the smallest things would set me off.

As I got older, I realized that a lot of my anger stemmed from the dysfunction of my home. Not so much from the teasing or name-calling from others. My rage was formulated by things that occurred in my life outside of school. I was never taught, or no one ever took time to help me understand how to cope with or handle my anger.

As I write, I contemplate all of the decisions I've made and the opportunities I wish I could have created back then. However, I understand that you are not able to change the past, but you can navigate the future. So, I wonder how I can help others who might be experiencing these same struggles. I understand entirely and challenge everyone to help me change the culture, especially in the black community. We can no longer teach that seeking counseling or psychological help is a sign of weakness. Strength and toughness are not just measured in the physical sense. We have to start teaching our youth that strength lies in the power of your mind. We have to fight to change and not fight for the destruction of one another.

Throughout my life, despite the tragedies I've faced, no one stopped to take us to a counselor or therapist, because this was a mark of weakness. It took me until I was in my late twenties for someone to show me that counseling helps. I mean, when I think about it, fighting almost daily, weekly or just frequently, to me, that's a major cry out for help. We have to fight not only to wipe the tears from their eyes but give them a solution that could potentially stop the crying.

I understand that we struggle to make things go viral daily, especially those things we find very amusing or like considerably. What if we start a challenge to get our youth into counseling. What if we put on our gloves to fight for change? I'm not talking about fighting to discuss it but fighting with actions. Let's fight to get our kids and adults into a counseling session to help them find ways to release their frustration.

Take me for an example, imagine the obstacles I could have avoided in my life if I was allowed to speak with someone to let out all of the things that were eating me up inside. Better yet, think about all of the school shootings that have taken place in America in the last three years alone. We are fighting incorrectly. We have to change the dynamics and remove this epidemic together.

When I first started this chapter, I told you that fighting is not always a bad thing; it depends on what, who, and why you are fighting. To increase your odds of winning a fight, you must understand the real purpose and vision for the fight. Fight for your job, but do not fight at your job (did that hit home?). Fight for that person who is special to you, but do not fight that person that is special to you. Most importantly, fight for our youth, and let's not fight them.

We can make a change, but we have to learn how to apply the correct fighting techniques. I once wore that stigma that has been placed on many of our youth, but I believed different. I was determined for different, and when I saw different, a change occurred. Just as I am sharing with you, more individuals are, will, or have experienced similar events in their lifetime. For those, it is time for a new fighting stance. I hope these words of encouragement provides you with the motivation to change.

CHAPTER 7

THOSE TWO GUYS

H ow did a lost boy like me find his way out; the answer is in this chapter. Have you ever had someone who was placed in your life, but you didn't understand why? When they are around, you wonder to yourself, why you? Why was this person in my life out of all people? I'm not sure I deserve, or I've earned the right to be in their presence; this is how I felt with the majority of the people I met at an early age. Especially, if they were extremely pleasant to me.

I was so used to dealing with people who had nasty attitudes and aggressive behavior. I dealt with the attitudes and anger issues so much that it shaped a part of my character. After being around those types of personalities for several years, you become numb to the lifestyle, and anything outside of it is abnormal. Fortunately for me, these two guys have made a significant impact on my life. Probably not until now, as they read this book, have they ever known their effects on me. These two men are my Uncle Donnie Carroll, aka "Patnik," and the man I call my second father, Dr. Alvin Chapman.

Let's start with my Uncle Donnie. He is the type of person who will bring life to any party and bring about laughter in any situation. His positivity enabled me to find a bright side in my life. Despite my differences, he never looked down on my inabilities, nor did he ever judge me for any mistakes I may have made. I honestly believe wholeheartedly that my uncle saw his brother mistreating me, but out of respect for his older brother, he kept quiet and provided support for me in ways that were safe for the both of us. No matter the situation I was facing, he would always magically appear.

For instance, in the year 2000, at my dad's house, I was entering the bathtub and slipped, and my head hit the toilet and broke it. My dad immediately ran in the bathroom and let it rip. He did not ask me if I was ok; he was more worried about the broken toilet.

Well, to make a long story short, he put me out of the house with my clothes in a trash bag. Guess who showed up, yep, my uncle. When I wanted to learn to shoot a basketball, he would leave work and come over to hang out with me to show me how to shoot. When I was trying to figure out how to do the dating thing, there was no father and son moment; it was an uncle and nephew thing. He taught me the importance of dressing with pride and introduced me to one of my favorite meals, eggs, and noodles (Do not knock it until you try it lol).

The way my uncle impacted my life, I could go on and on for days describing it. His organic care, love, and compassion gave me the strength to persevere throughout my youth days.

If you have ever followed me, been inspired by a speech I've given or read a book I've written (you will catch that one in a minute). It's all because of these two guys. There are no words to describe the impact each of them has had on me. However, I would do my best to paint a picture for you in this chapter. Let me tell you about the second one.

Dr. Alvin Chapman, a man, let me pause for a moment here (pause). My eyes fill with tears when I think about the impact this man has had on my life. Dr. Chapman is a man who knew nothing of me until probably midway of the 7th grade. He is the biological father of my best friend, my brother, and person blood couldn't make us any closer; Christopher Chapman. Through the connection I had with his son Chris, Dr. Chapman embraced me with love without even saying a word. He wiped tears from my eyes when I didn't realize I was crying. I was lost, I mean really lost in the world, from the gangs to feeling alone at home. My path was so dark, but God saw fit to align my walk to cross paths with the man who guided me through life with his actions, Dr. Chapman.

One of my greatest memories of my childhood was in the front yard of his home (well driveway) in Kathleen, Ga. I swore up and down that I was the man in basketball. I could jump, shoot, dribble; I was pretty good if you asked me ☺. One afternoon Chris and I were shooting outside, and here comes Dr. Chapman challenging the both of us against just him. I chuckled, of course, because in my mind, I was like this old man is not able to play ball.

I was talking mad trash; well, to make a long story short, he kicked our butts (lol). To make matters even worse, he ended the game with a shot that will forever be ingrained in my mind, an ole school hook shot. I'm still shaking my head when I think about it.

Basketball was just a fraction of what he has taught me. Through his actions as a father and as a husband, he gave me a view of something; I had never seen before. He cared for his family like nothing else in the world mattered. He openly cared for me and never once judged me on any of the things I may have done. He's never said it directly, but I know it to be true.

When I worked at Wendy's, he was one of the very few people that would at least once a week come by order and a chili and side salad. I believe wholehearted that this was his way of stopping in to check on me to see how I was doing. How did my schedule align with his visits, beats me, but I appreciated it greatly!

As I write and think about how everything has transpired in my life, I'm just blown away. Imagine being a young man in his late teens driving 19 miles one way to go and visit someone who is changing your life without you even knowing it. Everyone has that one person; you are probably thinking about them now.

They're that individual who, without having to say a word, showed you the love, care, and empathy you needed at that moment. If you have not found that person, they are there; you have to open your eyes and accept it. Sometimes they are the people who you see daily or once a month, but you often shut them down or ignore their messages.

Well, you could be shutting out the person who is supposed to lead you to your purpose. For those of you who know who these particular people are, please take a few minutes now to write a message to that special someone, thanking them for changing your life. It does not have to be too long, no need for a full essay, just a few lines to let them know you appreciate who they have been in your life.

Here are my notes:

Dear Uncle Donnie, thank you for caring for me and accepting me for who I am. No matter which way life blew me, in my mind, you were always in my corner. Thank you, Unc.

Dear Dr. Chapman, even though you made a mistake on the 1911 selection (inside joke for any Kappa's reading this), God did not make a mistake by positioning you to be a father figure to a boy in need. Words alone will never be enough to express my level of gratitude accurately;

however, I want you to know. From the bottom of my heart, I am eternally grateful for you and mom (Mona Chapman).

Lesson learned for this chapter:

No matter how tough life gets or what obstacles you have to overcome or what pain you have to endure, never give up. Always try to find the strength to live unselfishly. You will be amazed at the power you will gain from helping others. If you find yourself in a situation where someone is helping you, be hesitant to discourage help. You might miss out on your purpose.

Life is going to throw challenges at you, but you have to find that mentor, that trust buddy, who understands you more than you know. I know some of you are asking, how do you know if they are the right person to accept advice? Well, the best way I've learned to filter out people is by how they approach a situation. If a person approaches you with a directive mindset, they are most likely not the best for your growth. If a person comes to you openly with an attentive ear, then they are more likely to address your issues and not force their opinions on you.

The less they talk, the more they can listen.   Dr. Chapman never said a word about his contributions to my life. The fact that a person can do so many things to change your life without saying a word is a huge testament to their character.

CHAPTER 8

THE LIFE OF A SOLDIER

I have never really openly admitted to anyone until now that I had a learning disorder as a youth. My learning disability is also one of the reasons I never directly applied for college while in high school. In high school, I was always the kid behind in class. My comprehension skills were never on the same level as other students. I was a visual learner. If there was a demonstration, I could easily replicate it. If you gave me a book of instructions to read and comprehend the majority of the times, I was going to be unsuccessful.

I just could not overcome the challenges of my comprehension skills. It took me until I was in the 11th grade for a teacher to spend a few extra minutes studying me to notice my situation and see that it was a significant issue for me. If I was given a multiple-choice test, I would fail miserably. If you gave me the same test to work out and show my work, I would ace it every time, no problem. My teacher asked me to stay after school one day for an examination with another facility member to conduct a very similar exercise. It was confirmed at that moment that I had some form of testing disorder. What a sigh of relief for the math portion, but that did not account for my poor comprehension skills.

In the back of my mind, I knew where this disadvantage came from; I just had to find a way to overcome it. The poor comprehension skills came from the lack of support and encouragement in the value of reading at home. I came from a home where the importance of those skills was not stressed, so there was no support or guidance on how to overcome this obstacle. We were taught the value in life comes from hard work on a job. Reading was an afterthought.

As embarrassing as that was in high school, I knew I could not attend college with that level of comprehension. So, I never applied. Heck, I never even took the SAT nor the PSAT. It had already been proven that I was unable to pass a standardized test; why would I take myself through the misery of failing again. However, for me to get out of my environment, I knew I had to leave altogether.

College was no longer an option due to my testing inabilities and financial limitations. My income was not sufficient enough to pay for school nor enough to provide a decent living for my sister, brother, and me; so, I turned to the military. What I did not realize at the time was that for me to join the service, I had to take and pass a standardized test. Passing the examination required a minimum score of 31. I failed this exam three times!! I kept my efforts to join the service hidden from everyone because I was extremely embarrassed that I was unable to pass a standardized test.

When others found out about my plans to join the service, they assumed I was following the family norm. In my family, the bar was never set very high, in my opinion. Around me were workers of and for other people's dreams. I was making the same amount of pay as most adults around me while I was in high school.

I just knew there had to be more for me out there. I engraved it in my mind to never follow in the same footsteps as those I've seen. I was not spending the rest of my life working for someone else's dream to come true; I was destined to achieve my goals. Every day I would remind myself that I would not give in to the stigma of being ignorant to other opportunities in the world.

My plan was to go as far away from the captivity of my past life and find my way in the world. It was like a battle against the world. Obstacles were set in place along with turmoil and trouble, but only the strongest will survive (at least that's how I viewed it). So, I did exactly that! I left and went as far away as the service would let me. In that quest, whew, I've made so many mistakes, and I'm grateful for every one of them. I've met so many amazing people and have acquired many new friendships. Through my process, I've learned how to terminate relationships that were of no value to my life.

Throughout the journey, I was very wary as to how I would continue to overcome and choose the correct path to travel. How would I attend college aggressively while serving in the military? How would I progress through the ranks in the military to gain enough income to support my desires? I had seen very few who could show me the way, and with those few, it was still a long time for them to reach that point of completion, especially with college. Well, I finally embraced the fact that in this life, it is up to me to succeed or fail.

After my completion of basic training, I was sent for Advance Individual Training at Fort Gordon, Ga. Upon arrival at my new installation, I begin immediately to seek assistance from the education center on how to attend college. I applied for admission to Central Texas College (CTC). The enrollment process required a placement test. Boy, was I scared and nervous, but I passed on the first try.

After I completed the placement test, I had to wait until I made it to my primary duty station to enroll in my first actual course. The first course I took was in Algebra, and it was during my deployment to Iraq, well, I bombed it (no pun intended) badly.

Taking online courses required a different level of discipline and learning techniques that I had not mastered yet. It was already a struggle for me to learn inside of the classroom with a teacher teaching. Now I have to teach myself something new, using a device I knew nothing about; oh, my apologies, I left out that critical part, I didn't know how to use a computer until after I entered the military. In my household as a teenager, I was forbidden from using the computer inside the home. It was only for my stepmom.

After my first failed college attempt at CTC, I was discouraged and frustrated. It was like I was finally about to give in to the pressure of defeat. I was tired of failing at this education thing. I wanted more, but every time I felt like I was getting up, I would get hit with another right hook unexpectedly that knocked me back down. That failure

SHATTERPROOF: The Art of Perseverance 79

took a lot out of me. I was at the point where I honestly was considering throwing in the towel. What did I have to lose?

Everyone around me was living their lives in what seemed to be a happy state, but I'm struggling because of my differences. Why? Why continue to take yourself through the pain? That's the question I continued to ask myself every day and night. Well, something happened that probably should have kept me down, but God knows, there was a different fire lit when it happened.

Immediately following my course failure, I was selected to attend a company board. For those of you who not familiar with the military. A company board is an event where you compete against other members of your team for a chance to be recognized as the Soldier of the month or employee of the month. As I started preparing for the competition, I noticed that one of the deliverables for the event was, you had to write a letter as if you were in charge of the unit (First Sergeant).

When I saw this request, I was nervous at first. I wanted to win this board, so I gathered my thoughts started writing. This time, I did something completely different; I used two things I've never used before, a dictionary and a thesaurus. I knew if I wanted to win this, I had to bring something different. I would be embarrassed if I had to give someone something that I had written without researching writing techniques. For heaven's sake, my writing skills were probably barely on a high school level. This time I was eager to get to work. I spent countless hours working on the letter. I mean, I went all-in on it.

It was finally time for the leadership committee to read and consider the letters as the final stage for the competition. The feedback I received from the First Sergeant was beyond disrespectful. After reading the letter, he wrote and responded with, "there's no way you wrote this letter, someone else had to write it for you. It is written too well." In the words of my wife, "what in the whole hell, do you mean"? I was heated.

The entire room just looked around in expectation of me to flip out. Heck, as I write this, I can see why. How disrespectful! However, my reaction was different. I just stood there with my head held high while I was being belittled.

From that day forward, I made a vow to myself that I will learn something new every single day. I became determined never to give someone else's negativity enough power to make me feel that low ever again. I knew it was impossible to live a life without negativity, so I prepared myself to intake any form of negativity brought my way. If I was ready for the negativity, it is unable to conquer me. The reason I was so hurt when the First Sergeant said it to me was, I was unprepared for it. After that event, I learned to channel the negativity to fuel my actions for success.

As you are reading this book, you are probably facing obstacles full of negative energy from all of the no's, do not, cannot, and even insults you've heard. You are trying to figure out how do you overcome; better yet, how do you handle the situation? Do you lash out in retaliation? How do you suppress your anger amid frustration? Well, let me be the first, second, or third person to tell you that it is not an easy pill to swallow. However, when you master it, the benefits are much grander.

Take my scenario as an example. As a Soldier, you are taught a militant style of discipline. This means, when your supervisor or leader makes a statement, whether it is good, bad, sad, or just downright ignorant, you must suppress your feelings and not respond. Any feedback you provide regarding their comments could be considered disrespect. Disrespect in the service can result in a rank reduction, pay reduction, and Uniform Code of Military Justice (UCMJ) actions. Yes, it is brutal, I know. However, it taught me something that I want to share with you. What I learned from that type of mindset is to pivot as often as possible and use negativity as a source of engine fuel to propel you forward.

The more I was denied a well-deserved promotion, insulted for my lack of knowledge or discourage for my inabilities to function, the more strategic I became. I grind 10 to 20 times harder than anyone around me, and every day before my head hits the pillow, I've learned something new. I started reading while everyone else was asleep. I turned down the "Turn up music" and turned up the inspirational videos and quotes.

I began to separate myself from certain environments and people. I started to become closer to those from which

I could give and receive a great deal of knowledge. I would only accept and entertain mutual friendships. I became more selective about those around me. The reason being is, there's a deposit made from every person you meet. That deposit can be useful, or it could be harmful; however, you have to be able to discern the difference between the two. I started to observe more often, which opened my eyes to a lot of things. For me, everyone has a place in your life. It's up to you to properly place them.

For you, it's the same thing. Negative or positive, you have to learn to take control of every situation and maneuver the pieces of your puzzle to their correct spots. I call it, becoming a Solider in life. Learning how to use negative thoughts and not replace them. Allow them to fuel your momentum. I'm not telling you to surround yourself with all negativity, but you have to learn how to invite it in. I hear people say all of the time; I'm not surrounding myself with negative thoughts.

Well, the best way to defeat someone is to catch them off guard. If you are inviting it in and understand how to use it, T.I said it best, "You stay ready, so you don't have to get ready!". That's a factual statement. Those who do not understand how to use negativity are afraid of it and try to remove it. Let me ask a question if everything is moving at the same pace forward, how do you know if you've made progress?

Sometimes you have to invite negativity in to propel yourself forward for success. Caution: If you have not learned how to channel the negative energy, please hold off on the invitations. There are risks of being consumed with negativity if you do not understand how to use it effectively. However, when you have mastered channeling negative energy, then it's GAME TIME! Tell them or it to bring it on! For those of you who are seeking how to channel it, well you are in luck, I'm going to show how.

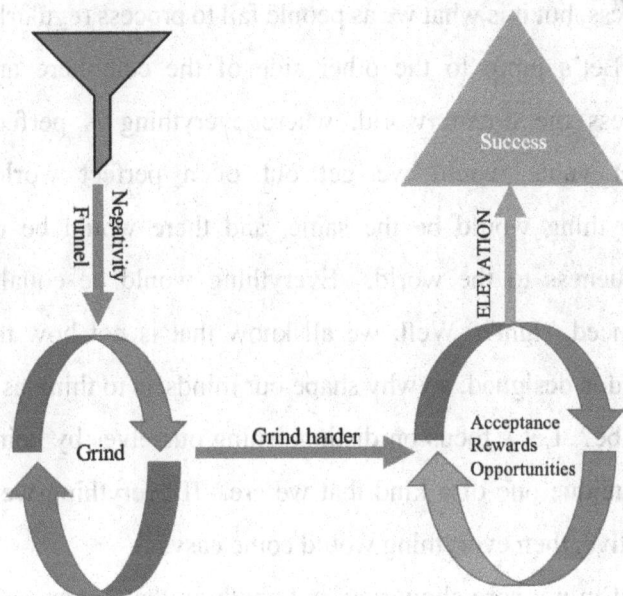

Note: Every successful person has a story or a trial that inspired them to keep pushing; you are included in that list. You will face and experience the no, don't, can't, shouldn't, and even various forms of insults in your lifetime. Avoiding those encounters is impossible. However, understanding how to process them is the key. The figure above is not rocket science, nor is it a mind-blowing process, but it is what we as people fail to process regularly.

Let's jump to the other side of the coin here and address the dream world, where everything is perfect. What value would we get out of a perfect world? Everything would be the same, and there would be no uniqueness to the world. Everything would be equally balanced, right? Well, we all know that is not how the world is designed, so why shape our mindsets to think as it will be? Let's focus on distinguishing ourselves by being the unique one of a kind that we are. If everything were positive, then everything would come easy.

I'm not sure about you, but anything that comes easy to me is also easy to leave. So, I say leave the easy stuff alone and face the challenges. Have you ever noticed that the things you work the hardest for you protect, value, and care for the most? Me too! Please do not get me wrong; positivity is crucial for you to stay encouraged. The secret to it all is, all positivity stifles your growth. You have to balance out the equation between positivity and negativity.

Having too much of just one is bad, but having the right amount is the formula for success.

This, my friend, is the reason why I kept and continue to allow negativity to come around. I have learned how to master the funneling process and boy what a joy it is to see the results.

CHAPTER 9

DETERMINATION

Most times, when people see or read about "successful" individuals, they wonder to themselves, what and how did they reach that level in their lives. What separates or differentiate them from me? Is it the myth that only specific races and ethnicities are given a big break? Or maybe the skin I'm in is inferior to others. The first thing you need to understand is success has no color, and it sees no color. Regardless of your race, gender, or ethnicity, you can achieve all the things you have a desire to achieve. The real question is, are you determined?

To be successful in anything in life, you must first define what does success means to you. To you, it might mean being rich, and to someone else, it might mean being wealthy. Is there a difference? Absolutely! These are terms we've been taught to use to describe a class of wealthy, without really understanding their specific meaning. It is our job as individuals to become and remain determined to gain as much knowledge as possible to progress forward for success. We have to stop using the same terminology to define completely different things.

Let's go off track for a quick moment. The term rich defines a person with a plethora of money and no real strategy or plan on how to use it. A wealthy individual has an abundance of funds that continuously grow and make more money. The terms used to describe your success makes a difference. When you encounter wealthy individuals, which there are plenty of them, you will never hear them refer to themselves as rich. Why? The hidden secret is above, there is a different meaning to the term rich, and it is not a positive one. I know you are probably wondering, why am I discussing money in a determination chapter, well the truth is, I have yet to meet a person who did not want to increase their revenue or person income ☺. So, I figured why not bridge the gap here. The key to an abundance of wealth is determination.

Regardless of whether you are seeking financial or professional growth, or maybe you are striving to be a better parent or just a better person in general, it all starts and continues with determination. Determination is the mental and physical will to pursue a goal or desire with all your efforts. It is relentlessly facing any and every obstacle ahead with fierce tenacity, passion, and a never defeated attitude.

As a youth and teenager, I heard the word "no" so much that it almost became the beginning and end of every sentence. The no's turned into, you shouldn't, that's dumb, you are making a big mistake. You are probably nodding your head in agreement because people have said the same or similar things to you in your life. The truth is, the world is full of people who will try to discourage you and distract you from your vision.

People who are insecure or visionless will always try to cloud someone else's vision. When this happens, you have to learn how to navigate the waters of haters and persevere to your goal; that happens with determination. I remember while in high school, a young man asked me in front of my dad, what I wanted to do after I graduated. I told him I'm going to be a dentist, an orthodontist, to be exact. I'm going to own my practice. I had it laid out. I was going to go to Albany State with my best friend and major in chemistry.

Well, my dad jumped in immediately, saying, "no, you are not; you have to go into the military; college is not going to pay your bills. I'm not paying for no college." I know you are probably thinking that is dream shattering, well for me, it was not! I didn't have any dreams and still don't have any, I have goals. Dreams are for those who sleep. Dreams, for me, were never in the picture. I figured, if I'm dreaming, I'm not able to move forward. I've never heard of anyone accomplishing their goals while sleeping. So, I figured if the only way I can have a dream is to sleep, I rather not have one.

I accepted his statement as fact, but only the portion about him was not paying for my education. As for anything else, he had and still has no control over my destiny. I was determined to achieve my goals, no matter what, and to do so without ever asking him for a dime. You see, sometimes, we have to move strategically. We cannot always be bothered and thrown off by someone else's lack of support and fears.

It's not up to someone else to believe in your goal. You are the only one that has to believe. So, for me, I took that mindset and completed four degrees by the age of 31, achieved a successful career in the United States Army, and formed two very successful companies. All of which did not require the belief, permission, nor acceptance of doubters. It just needed me to believe in myself and be determined.

Now, when I am in a conversation with other executives and business owners, they asked, what if they don't give us the opportunity. That's funny to me. With my life experiences, I've learned to not look for someone to give me an opportunity I make my own. I've learned, if someone gives you something, they can easily control that part of you. You have to make a conscious effort never to allow someone to put you in a puppet show. You have to manage your journey. Take a minute and look at the figure below. I would like for you to process it for a second.

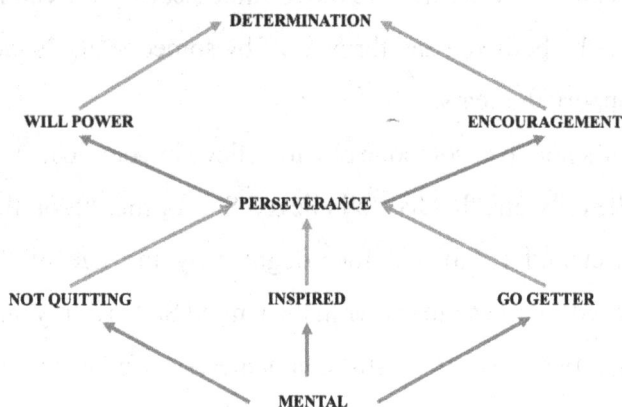

DETERMINATION

WILL POWER   ENCOURAGEMENT

PERSEVERANCE

NOT QUITTING   INSPIRED   GO GETTER

MENTAL

Note: The foundation of determination evolves from your mindset. Your mental state drives all of your actions in life. Being successful is no difference. Having a strong mental foundation will enable you to persevere and remain determined to pursue and achieve your desired goals.

The figure above depicts the anatomy of determination. At the root of determination is **Mentality**. Everything starts with a mindset. The mental state of an individual has to consist of an unwavering attitude. Your mentality is focused on **Not Quitting**.

Never give up on a goal or a desire. No matter how challenging the task of overcoming the obstacle may seem. Always be **Inspired**! On your quest to success, no one should believe in you more than you. You have to be inspired to accomplish something or things that are greater than your current state. As you are inspired, you have to be a **Go-Getter**! Waiting on someone to give you a handout or repay what you believe they owe you will leave you stuck waiting. Never wait on someone else to move, you move and have them to catch up; stay hungry for growth.

Your mindset will transform into the **Perseverance** phase. Sacrifices, trials, and tests will accompany this transformation. This transformation is where you, as an individual, will be forced to find the courage to remain on course. You will have to find the **Will Power** and **Encouragement** to accomplish the goals you set out to achieve, even if it means encouraging yourself. You have to root for you even if no one else will. All of these efforts, my friend, is "**DETERMINATION**."

At an early age, I was written off to the streets and justice systems by family members, neighbors, and peers. Even statistically, I had no future. By the age of 20, I should have been incarcerated, prosecuted for domestic violence, or some form of gun violence. I was surrounded by other people's negative energy and perspective of my character. However, my vision and purpose were different.

I believed my life was created for much more, but words alone were not sufficient enough to convince and challenge the minds of the masses. I had to reshape my mentality to inspire myself, that no matter what I face going forward, I would not quit. I will go after and obtain any and everything that is meant for me. I will persevere even when those around me wanted to tear me down. My faith and determination are my cornerstones in life, and I want to encourage you to find the same.

No matter what the obstacle is or how big the task **<u>You</u> <u>Can Accomplish IT</u>**! Losing everything at an early age gave me every reason to quit. Having faith and determination gave me every reason to keep going. God predestined something more significant for my life, and the same is true for your life; be determined to follow your calling.

CHAPTER 10

THE INFECTIOUS "NO" and "CAN'T"

From a young age to an elderly adult, we all have experienced hearing the terms "no" and "can't." Maybe it was something that you wanted, desired, or simply something you needed, but others around you were unable to see or believe in the same vision, principle, or thought. I know I've experienced it so many times in life; even while I'm writing this book, I'm still experiencing those words.

Hearing those terms for so long was like an infectious virus or cancer that would spread throughout my body every time I would listen to them. People say words cannot hurt you, but I say that's a lie. There's power in the tongue of any human being. Take the terms "no" and "can't." When they are ingrained in you from an early stage, they become more than just words. They can act as a cancerous cell that can destroy the hopes, dreams, and goals of anyone who submits to them. Let me explain.

From the times we were toddlers, we've been told: no, can't, stop, and many other halting terms. All of which would translate later into, cannot, unable, or not going to happen, which are barriers preventing forward progress from being made. These words are the root of negative thinking, preventing you from being successful.

They are instilled in us at an early age, and as years progress forward, the reaction to those words become more like muscle memory when we hear them. It becomes a habit to stop when we hear the term no immediately. We slow down our progress or reduce our efforts when we hear the word can't. The "no" from someone else transforms into "can't" in your mind, and now another barrier is formed. Maybe someone tells you, you can't complete a particular task or that you are incapable of doing something. This attempt to deter you is something I know all too well; let me share this story with you.

I was raised in a family that lacked the knowledge of understanding how powerful and essential college is when you are striving for success. The majority of the people within my immediate circle lacked any advanced education. For the majority, high school education was a stretch. Due to their lack of knowledge, they devalued the efforts of others who sought a higher level of education. It was as if pursuing a higher goal in life that exposed me to different environments was a threat to them.

When I wanted more out of life or wanted to strive for greater, someone around me would try and force their fears on me and say you can't do that. If "can't" wasn't their answer, "no" was next in line as one of their responses. Their fears and lack of ambition became a barrier to my journey at a very young age. I was a teenager that had been through a pretty significant amount of trauma and with limited exposure to anything outside of my immediate surroundings.

I was prohibited from going and hanging out with other kids my age, so my development socially was reduced. The adults around me were mostly employed by the local retail, trucking, and other similar occupations. The lack of effort from others not pursuing a higher career created a genuine tempting offer for me to settle. However, I refused to give in to the peer pressure. I was going to be successful no matter what obstacles laid ahead of me. I was determined not to allow others discouraging words and actions to prevent me from continuously believing in and encouraging myself.

It is strange how the idea of me becoming successful created so many negative thoughts, even biblically. Yes, bible scriptures were used to try and discourage me from advancing (chuckle). I remember shortly after the conversation with my dad; I coincidently got a biblical lecture from my grandmother about how it's easier for a cow to enter the eye of a needle than it is for a rich man to enter the gates of heaven! That's crazy, in my opinion. Your success does not determine your faith, religion, or afterlife. Your class of wealth doesn't even always determine success. However, this was another "no" and "can't" tactic. Their approach was extremely strange and still is as I think about it. Being successful for some reason was more taboo than it was an honor or rewarding.

When that mindset surrounds you, it is challenging not to give in to the pressure of others' opinions; let alone challenge the norm. During high school, the pressure almost took over me. I was frustrated by not having the support and encouragement from those around me. I was fed up with being an outcast. I was seeing everyone within my circle, drinking, smoking, and being the so-called life of the party. Why was I still looking in from the outside? I wanted to be a part of a popular group.

One day while in school, I broke. I walked out of the classroom and went straight into the principal's office and asked to be withdrawn from school. Yes, I was attempting to drop out of school just a year before graduation. I was stuck, tired, and completely overwhelmed with negative emotions. I was not grasping all the concepts from class, and my perception of others who had dropped out seemed so enticing.

Well, while in the office, my assistant principal was about to give me the papers to process the withdrawal, and something hit me. It seemed as if he was telling me I did not belong, or I could not cut it. The assistant principal response may have been a form of reverse psychology, but I believed differently. When I saw his response, I started to think about me being the dumb kid in class. The different boy that no one found valuable, the less popular kid whose only choice after school would be the military. All these thoughts ran through my mind, and I asked myself, why not me?

As soon as that question came to my mind, I decided to gather myself, stand up, and walk out of the office. I returned to class, and things were on. In the midst of a negative situation, the doubt and lack of support forced me to channel the, no, don't, can't, and unable into why not me and push. When I left school that same day, I went to work at my favorite job, Wendy's (lol). Dr. Chapman came to the drive-thru and ordered his usual.

It was very strange, because every time I saw him, it was like he would deposit some energy and encouragement into my spirit without even talking about any issues. Those deposits kept me moving and driving forward. It built a level of confidence that others are often threatened by and might misconstrue as arrogance. Whether someone calls it arrogance or confidence, it doesn't matter to me. I believe in my abilities and trust that they will never fail me. I stopped listening to other people's opinions of me and started walking and speaking with confidence in myself.

When I made the decision to go for it all and not worry about what others thought anymore, I wrote a reminder in a small notepad. It stated, "my life will be different no matter the cost or what others think about me." This message encouraged me and elevated me to different levels. My environment was terrible, so I started working 40 hours plus consistently.

If I had any extra time before my shift at Wendy's, I would go to Jack O's barbershop and sweep up hair. The owner would pay me a little cash, but hey, it kept me away from the negativity of my environment. When I got selected for a job at Target, I tried to work as late as possible. This way, all I had to do was go to the house to sleep; social interaction would be minimal. I was destined to change my outcome and environment, by any means necessary.

What am I trying to convey to you in this message? At some point in life, you must stop worrying and caring about what others are going to think about you. People are going to have their opinions no matter what you do in life. What you must remember is, their opinions are not your reality. Only you can determine your reality and outcome, so take control.

Accept the fact that you are going to face MANY no's and can't situations, but just because someone says no to your goal or vision, that does not mean you have to stop striving to accomplish it. Just say screw it! If everyone around is saying no, can't, and I shouldn't, but you can look yourself in the mirror and say "yes" and "you can," turn up with it, and go for it all!

Someone else's GPS does not guide your destination, you have your own roadmap, and you are free to travel any direction you want.   Never allow someone else's pessimistic thinking and attitude impact your optimism. Let them think small, while you think big and kick butt. If they call you arrogant, accept it with a smile, and continue to be confident!

CHAPTER 11

FAITH

T he key to overcoming and achieving any task assigned to you lies within your own beliefs and convictions. It is the belief and conviction that something will occur without having any physical evidence that it will; this is what we call faith. Faith has and still is what equipped me to persevere through all different forms of adversity.

Whether it was tragedy, loneliness, bullying, or others lacking the faith in me, my faith was my rock.

You have to believe in yourself regardless if others believe in you or not. You have to have enough faith in yourself that you will overcome the challenges that life will bring you. Notice, I said will. Life will bring you challenges, and it is your job not to waiver from your belief. You have to stand steadfast in your faith that no matter what, I can and will achieve greatness. You have to gain control of your thoughts and your emotions. All of which is done by having faith.

Take, for example, a person's belief that working hard daily on a job will provide them with the opportunity to obtain a pay raise. They have to have the faith to believe that this will take place in order for them to keep pushing harder and harder each day. If they do not think the concept of working harder will render a pay increase, then their faith is structured to believe just as such. It does not matter how you formulate the equation; the standard variable will always be faith. The common variable that you can put into any equation and get the desired results you want from it is faith. Now, note, I did not say immediately, but with faith, all things are possible.

Let's breakdown the formula for faith a little more to ensure we have a clear understanding before I share my faith journey. The faith formula can operate in positivity or negativity. Take a negative faith formula, for instance. If you have convinced yourself and believe that something will not happen, you will be reluctant to put forth more than minimum efforts into your actions.

In your mind, extra efforts are a waste of time and pointless. Especially when your faith has convinced your mind that you will fail or not succeed. It's strange how we often speak negativity into a situation and then wonder why nothing positive comes from it. Having positive faith versus negative faith makes a huge difference. What matters, even more, are positive actions and not words. Words alone will never be able to bring you all that you need, but faith while doing the work will.

Now let's modify the formula some here and bring some positivity into it. Let's replace "that will never happen" with "I can, or I will" or "it can, or it will." Those words should make you feel proud and fully capable of completing any and everything you desire.

As I mentioned earlier, words alone will never give you all that you need; however, it can encourage and provide momentum to propel you forward. We are all fortunate to believe and think what we want, so why spend your energy on the negative thinking and entertaining the foolishness of those who have a desire to bring you down. Create your faith formula with positive thinking and enjoy your happiness.

Let's talk about my faith journey for a few minutes. Statistically speaking, I should be serving a pretty long sentence in prison or dead due to violence. I know you are probably questioning why I would say such harsh things? Well, the truth is, studies have shown that African Americans are more likely to be exposed to multiple acts of violence at a very young age.

Adding to that statistic, kids who are exposed to gun violence or experience domestic violence are over 40% more likely to commit similar or more violent crimes. I was exposed to each of those categories, extreme violence, domestic violence, and gun violence. In my case, the statistics were wrong. I am no different from anyone else. I just had faith in myself that my past did and will not represent my future. What I hope it shows others is, with faith, you can create your future. We are not able to choose how our lives start and finish, but we can dictate what happens while we are in this life.

From the day my mother was murdered, I committed to doing things differently. To be better for my brother and my sister. If there were a chance that my mother could see us again from heaven, I would want her to be joyful and proud of what she sees. Making her proud was and still is my goal in everything I strive to accomplish. The challenge comes from when others try to steer you in a different direction. But it is my faith that keeps me on track to achieve that goal. In this world, none of us were promised an easy journey. But one thing is for sure; we will all have a journey in this world. It is up to us as individuals on how we navigate that journey.

Words are for inspiration, and actions are for confirmation. What do I mean by this statement? Well, on your journey, you will have challenges that will take you to your breaking point. It is at this breaking point that you will no longer be able to just speak words to make a difference; you will have to apply actions to make a difference. I was 17 years old when I arrived at my breaking point. I was too strong to be broken by the negativity within the house and too determined to fall deeper into the traps of the world. I learned at that age, that words were no longer impactful to my existence and that they will not carry me into the future. I was at a point in my life where I had to choose the path for my life. I could follow everyone else or lean on my faith. My belief has always been, I was made different for a reason. My job was to figure out what that reason was.

Even if I had to walk, run, claw, and fight my way through, I was up for the battle. My conviction was and still is, nothing will break me. I have a purpose, and not until that purpose is fulfilled will I give in or quit. After experiencing living life without my mother and seeing her beg others for assistance, it taught me to put my faith in myself when striving to succeed. Never to put yourself in a situation where your life lies in the hands of another individual. The truth of the matter is, no one will ever care for you like you do. We all have our own desires, and it is almost impossible to find someone who will sacrifice their journey so that you can accomplish yours.

We can no longer wait for someone else to give out because eventually, you will give up. You have to invest and believe in yourself and know that all is achievable with your faith. If you want a positive outcome, structure your faith formula with a positive variable. If you want a pessimistic lifestyle, structure your faith formula with negative factors, and you will get your desired outcome. The choice is yours. Invest in you; however, you feel the need and watch your FAITH orchestrate your actions!

CHAPTER 12

THE ART OF PERSEVERANCE

Before I dive too deep into this final chapter, I want to take the time to say thank you to all of my readers. The fact that you are reading this message means you have taken the time out of your schedule to dedicate to hearing my story. Thank you for spending the time to allow me the opportunity to share my journey with you. I'm eternally grateful and hope that one or more of my stories have inspired you or given you the courage to tackle any form of adversity you may be experiencing. Please ensure you read the entire book to the final page; there's a surprise just for you.

On this journey, we call life; we will all face similar and different situations that will try with every attempt to prevent and stop us from accomplishing our goals. The truth is, challenges are inevitable. I want you to accept that fact and prepare yourself not for the "if" it happens, but for the "when" it happens. There's not a single book in this world that can give you the blueprint for your life and predict all of the obstacles you will face. You have to prepare your mind and body for your personal journey. As authors, we share our stories to give you something to reference while you are on your journey. We all have a story to share, including you, never be afraid to write it down ☺.

What I've learned is, you have to appreciate the struggles in life. The accomplishments, fame, glamour, and money are not the things that shape our character; those items build facades. It is our trials, struggles, down-falls, and stumbles that genuinely form the elements of our character. Let no one convince you into believing that life will be easy…that's a lie.

At some point in life, you will fall and get knocked down. You will be required to get into the trenches and fight. Accept it and prepare yourself for the battle. Battles are typically lost by those who are caught in the element of surprise. Defeat will conquer those who are unprepared and surrender to those who are prepared and determined. As you continue to fight, you may have to wear the bumps and bruises of the battle. You may even find yourself wearing shame, but trust me, there is nothing to be ashamed of; that's your journey! The tears, rips, and dirt are just colors for your story.

As you continue your journey, (because I know you will) prepare yourself to push with all of your strength. Dig deeper than you've ever dug before to accomplish whatever it is that your heart desires. For me, it was embracing my differences and defeating the odds. I knew that my troublesome past would bring along a lot of doubts. It even at times, generated doubts within me. However, when I learned to embrace and accept me, I begin to gain a new level of confidence in me and my faith. Despite what others around me said or thought, I was finally in control of my destiny and my future.

I had to learn how to fight differently, which was a valuable lesson for me. Fighting is not always with your fist. You have to learn to be intentional and smart about your fights. The first step for me was to master the concept of "be slow to speak and fast to listen;" this applies to any situation. You will be amazed at what you will find out about a person within the first 30-seconds. I challenge you to use this on your job, at school, at home, apply it anywhere. You will grateful that you did!

At an early age, statistics and even family members attempted to write my life story for me. Dead by the age of 20 years old or incarcerated for gun violence, or completely submerged into the gang activities. When the odds are against you, it is easy to conform to the thoughts and ideas of others. Accept their characterization of you as the norm. I'm grateful that God has given me the faith that I needed to persevere and the ability to truly identify who I am and my purpose.

It does not matter where you come from; we are all made equally. It's our determination that separates us. I truly believe that handouts are designed to be taken away, but hard work is intended to be kept. What does that mean? Never wait for someone to give you an opportunity, create your own!

The real Art of Perseverance lies within the individual, not in a concept or model. You are unique for a reason; embrace it. What if I would have given up in 1998 when my mother was killed? What about in 2005 when the exact same thing happens again to my cousin? What about if I was too prideful to learn how to properly read because of the thoughts of others around me? Perhaps, I should have left school on my attempt to drop out? Being lost in the world would have been easy for me; it is what people expected from me. The Art of Perseverance is what I'm grateful for the most. God created me with the unique ability to carry heavy burdens that are unbearable for others, all to be used as a living testimony that you are more than what the people in the world say and see.

There will always be what-ifs, especially when you are looking for success. You will hit hardships and pitfalls, but your goal and purpose have to be larger than the trial. Your faith has to be grounded and consumed with a fire that knows you will succeed. Your formula for success has to accept negativity and channel it to propel your desires and passions. You have to persevere. Nothing in this world is promised except the fact of not succeeding if you do not try.

I'm unable to guarantee you multi-million or billions of dollars, but what I can promise you and ensure you of is, life does not stop for anyone or anything, so why should you. If you do not persevere or exhibit courage, you will never know your possibilities. The Art of Perseverance is not about the significant wins on the other side. It's about knowing what's inside of you. You pushed yourself to your highest limits, and now you know what you can achieve!

CHAPTER 13

JUST US

Ever since Memorial Day of 1998, people have often wondered about the three kids who experienced such tragedy. I recently went to visit our old home and the house where my mother was murdered. Upon my arrival, an elderly lady came outside when she saw me; she immediately began to cry. I was amazed that after all those years, she remembered my brother, sister, and I. She told me she often asked around to see if anyone knew whatever happened to us. When she could finally gain herself, she walked over to me and just hugged me tightly. She told me she replays that event over and over in her head, wondering why things could not have been different. As I told her, we spent years wondering the same thing. Fortunate for us, my mother was able to deposit something in us that would carry us far beyond the world's imagination.

My brother and I have completed college with multiple degrees, and my baby sister has recently completed her bachelor's. We are preparing now to send her to Physician Assistant (PA) school. We are blessed to have a bond so strong and deeply rooted. We understand our past, and we embrace it fully. It's not always easy, but we are each other's strength, and that keeps us going. No amount of weight in this world is strong enough to break it. We face all adversity with confidence and determination. As struggle comes, we welcome it with open arms. When you can withstand the enemy face to face, the tables immediately turn in your favor.

We've decided to dedicate this chapter to our mother and share it with the world. We hope that our story touches others to make a difference and understand, no matter what life throws at you, be prepared to fight back. The world let me introduce you to, Just Us, the three who defied the odds.

In order from left to right: (left) Gene A. Carroll III,
(middle) Dr. Kendrick R. Carroll, (right) Amie V. Wimberly.

From Gene,

Dear Mama,

It's been a long time since we've spoken but I still remember the good days we had together. You made the simplest things feel so special and memorable. Unfortunately, God saw fit to bring you home early in life, but he blessed us with ways of remembering you. You have 4 grand babies, 3 from me and 1 from Kendrick, and none from Amie at this time. We want to make sure she has her career started before she has any. I named Denise after you and she has a happy spirit just like you! Daniyah provides comfort to me when I visit you, just like you did many times for me. Your grandson Gene is new to this world, but I am sure he will have some resemblance of you as well. My lovely wife Keshema has been the most supportive woman since you went home. I just want to say thank you for the foundational ethics and morals you instilled in me. I am doing my best to make you proud! I have kept my word of being there for Kendrick and Amie whenever they needed someone and promise to continue to do so. I miss you a lot and sometimes it is hard, but I know you are always with me in spirit! I can't wait until I am able to see and hug you again! I love you and I promise to continue striving to be the best man you could ever raise!

With love,
Your son Gene Autry Carroll III

BRENDA MOSLEY
WIMBERLY
DEC. 7. 1965
MAY. 25. 1998

From Kendrick

To My First Love, Mom,

I'm not really sure where to start it's been 21 years since I last heard your voice or felt your touch. As the tears roll down my face, I just think about all the times I wish I could just hear your voice. I miss you so much. You have two handsome grandsons and two beautiful granddaughters now. Gene and I are both married to two beautiful women who have really filled in to protect our hearts and care for us in ways that would make you proud as a mother in law. Gene is doing an awesome job as a big brother for us. Amie is still our innocent baby and the world still revolve around her to us. She is doing so well! We are so proud of the young lady she has become and continue to be. As for me, well I've found a different way of fighting nowadays. I'm actually heavily involved in business and technology with a focus on creating career opportunities for others.

I'm truly grateful for everything you did and still doing for me. Every day I use a gift or talent you have blessed me with. For years, I suppressed my thoughts and feelings in efforts to just push forward in life; but I realized that one of my gifts is involved in sharing our story with world. Now, I understand the reason for all of those trips you took me on to service your patients. It was another way of showing me how to help others. So, I'm going to do my best to do exactly that.

I'm looking forward to seeing and hearing your voice again. Until then I will continue to be the best man I can. I hope you are proud of the man I've become. Forever and always, I LOVE YOU with everything in me, Mom!

Your baby boy,
Dr. Kendrick R. Carroll aka Shard

BRENDA MOSLEY
WIMBERLY
DEC. 7. 1965
MAY 25. 1998

From Amie

To my angel,

For starters I want to say I love you and that there's not a day that goes by that I don't think about you. I wonder what you were like and how things would be if you were here. It's crazy to think how people often take for granted the time they have with their loved ones or how easily someone can rip them away. A mother is an irreplaceable person in a child's life, and I miss you every day. I remember when I was younger, and I went to camp to learn how to deal with grief. I learned that it helped to write things down and if it was personal, you could burn it. It sounds crazy but I thought when I burned the letters, the ashes would float up to you in Heaven and whatever I told you would be our secret. I grew up with a loving family but somethings you just needed you mother for. Being a girl, I think about the moments I'll never get to share with you such as looking for a wedding dress, asking for boy advice or just knowing you're only a phone call away whenever I need to talk. At my graduation, they asked for parents of the graduates to stand and I couldn't look up. The thought of you missing an important moment in my life hurt. I try not to cry much because I like to think that you're in a better place but sometimes the pain is just overbearing. I miss you mom and I wish you were here, but I know you're in Heaven looking down on me. I hope you're proud of the woman I am becoming, and I love you dearly.

Love,

Amie

BRENDA MOSLEY
WIMBERLY
DEC. 7. 1965
MAY 25. 1998

Homes in Twiggs County

This image is our home and where my mother husband committed suicide after he murdered her.

This image is our home and where my mother husband committed suicide after he murdered her.

This image is of the home of my grandma where my mother was murder. This is the final place where I saw my mother as she laid lifeless on the floor inside the gray storm door.

This image is of the home of my grandma where my mother was murder. This is the final place where I saw my mother as she laid lifeless on the floor inside the gray storm door.

THANK YOU FOR YOUR CONTINUED SUPPORT!

DR. KENDRICK CARROLL, DBA

9780578646718